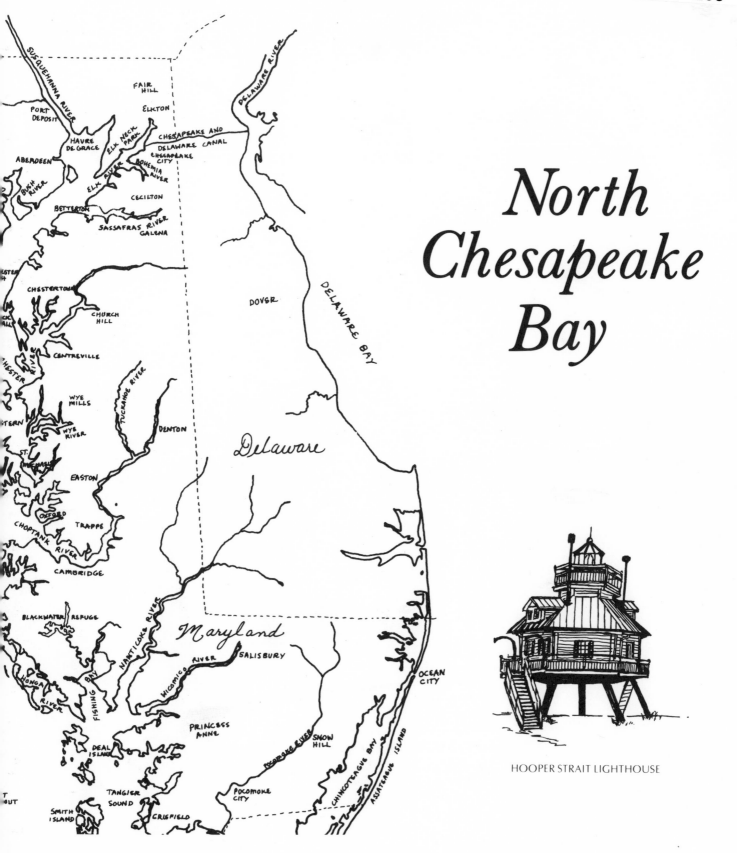

North Chesapeake Bay

HOOPER STRAIT LIGHTHOUSE

Illustrated by Barbara H. Hamer

FOUR SEASONS OF THE CHESAPEAKE BAY

About the cover

Along almost any creek of the Chesapeake Bay is a sunken boat, no less the cypress swamp of the Nassawango Creek near Snow Hill, MD.

First Printing — November, 1980
Second Printing — September, 1983

SUNRISE AT BOXTREE LANDING, MACHIPONGO, VA

FOUR SEASONS OF THE CHESAPEAKE BAY

RED HAMER Author-Photographer
BARBARA HAMER Associate Editor-Illustrator

Volume I
Spring-Summer Edition

Printed By
Taylor Publishing Company
Dallas, Texas, Malvern, PA

Published By
Four Seasons Book Publishers
P.O. Box 222
West Chester, PA

The First All-Color Pictorial of the Entire Chesapeake Bay

ACKNOWLEDGMENTS

We gratefully acknowledge the aid of the following persons in compiling this first-ever totally color portrait of the Chesapeake Bay:

David and Eleanor Baker, Wittman, Maryland, who welcomed us into their handsome plantation house, Webley — a gesture that saved us from the seven watch dogs.

Olga Crouch, of Elk Neck, Maryland, for information on her famed mother, Fannie May Salter, "Lady of the Lamp" at Turkey Point Light.

Charles and Verdie Eberle, Annapolis, and Edward LaDrew, Downington, Pa., who printed our photographs until they were literally blue in the face.

Lester Eckman, who loaned me his dock on North East Creek, Maryland, his Boston whaler and his knowledge of the North East River.

Bob Fears, deputy sheriff of Eastville, Virginia, who gave us a big welcome (Fears is 6-foot-7) and a list of fishermen with boats.

Howard Fellows, owner of the Kitty Knight House, Georgetown, Maryland, who provided us with provocative information, and who ate a cold dinner because of it.

Flora Gick, who made our research in North East, Maryland a bit easier.

R. James Holt, director, and his efficient executive assistant Nancy Sumner, at the Chesapeake Bay Maritime Museum, for their invaluable assistance.

The public relations ladies at the U.S. Naval Academy who are efficient, knowledgeable and pleasant . . . and drummed up a pass for the commencement exercises on 24 hour notice.

The management of Longfellows Restaurant, St. Michaels Harbor, who put up with our dinghy on their dinghy dock all summer.

Members of the Maryland Department of Natural Resourecs at Calvert Cliffs, Elk Neck State Park, Blackwater Wildlife, Refuge and Janes Island State Park whose informative guides were a tremendous help.

Brian and Jallan Gregg, St. Michaels, who looked after our boat, Casablanca, when we were on assignment.

Mrs. Howard Ketterman, pastor's wife, who voluntarily showed us around Crisfield and called ahead to the people we wanted to photograph.

Neal Kimmel, division manager of the Fine Books Division, Taylor Publishing Co., for his personal involvement and attention to fine detail.

Roland Lomax, St. Michaels, who took us on his fishing boat on an early morning crabbing expedition which netted photos of osprey, mute swan and very few crabs because it was cold and windy.

The Stapleforte Neilds, of Taylor's Island. who provided the view from the widow's walk.

James Byron (Mr. Jim) Richardson, one of the few remaining of America's great wood boat builders, who graciously spent hours from his work to tell us of the lore of the Eastern Shore.

Harry C. Rhodes, former superintendent of Queen Anne County schools, for background information on Queenstown, Maryland.

Elmer Riggin, model boat builder, who told us of the early days in the crabbing port of Crisfield, Maryland.

Larry Smith, captain of Wilma's Idea, a 41-foot Egg Harbor Motor Yacht that carried us into position to photograph the start of the Annapolis-to-Bermuda race.

Pat Smith, tour director of Historic Annapolis, Inc., who took us on a personal viewing of the William Paca House, Annapolis.

Inez Thompson, Rock Hall, who dredged up schedules of happenings around the Bay in general and Chestertown in particular.

Mrs. Cecile Turner, owner of the famed plantation house, Kendall Grove, near Eastville, Va., for her gracious hospitality.

Gary Van Hoven, who provided all the details on the Annapolis to Bermuda race.

Lem Ward, wood carver emeritus, who took us into his Crisfield, Maryland home sight unseen to observe and photograph the works that have him admired and famous in his 84 years.

Flo Maxwell, keeper of Hudson's Pharmacy, St. Michaels, who assured us every morning the world was in the right place, and that Barry Goldwater was coming to town Saturday.

Contents

First Printing • Nov. 1980
(10,000 copies)
Second Printing • Sept. 1983
(5,000 copies)
Third Printing • Oct. 1985
(5,000 copies)

THE BAY'S TROUBLED WATERS

Those of us who have cruised the rivers, coves and yawning expanses of the Chesapeake Bay have come to realize we have been some place special. We have not come to realize what it takes to keep it that way. Nor do we have the resolution to do so. Because of this fact of life . . . and of death . . . there is trouble brewing in these waters.

The trouble is deep down and, the trouble is, we cannot see deep down. The Chesapeake Bay is filled with the poisons of industry, the chemicals of farming sprays, silt from the stormy runoffs of banks plowed too close to the water, of oil spills and waste disposal accidents.

Millions of dollars are being spent on testing the water to see which part of the Chesapeake is worse off. A head law has been thrust upon the boat owner but, alas, government has put the cart before the horse. Few places have been made available to dump the stuff.

Factions, meanwhile, fight over who is the worst culprit. Who made the Chesapeake "old muddy," its stones and rocks polished with a coat of green goo? If you believe the offenders, the ducks did it.

Perhaps this is not the place for a dissertation on bay pollution. Perhaps we should permit the "Save the Bay" proponents to do all the work. No, I think it helps for the attack to come from another quarter — from as many quarters as possible — to put the pressure on government and industry to get God's blue earth cleaned up.

We took 3,700 photographs for this spring-summer volume before the editing began, and it occurred to us that while photographs can preserve the beauty of the Bay in our minds, only decent people can keep it beautiful. But it is not only a question of beauty. If we do not care for this great bay it will die, and all that lies around it — and in it — will also die.

Pollution is so insidious that one hardly knows what it is or from whence it comes. But sometimes it is blatant — when I see oil slicks in St. Michaels Harbor, or read that a waste disposal plant has accidentally dumped into the Choptank, or that the beaches of Kent Island are oil covered thanks to a tanker, or that the Sassafras is more polluted than ever. When these things are allowed to happen I worry about our bay.

My concern set in four years ago one midnight ride in a canoe high up on the Susquehanna River near Three Mile Island. Bubbles and an oil substance could be seen clearly under a full moon, and the profusion at mid river was never ending.

I thought of these midnight polluters and their impact the following summer when a little girl gulped some water in the North East River in upper Maryland and died of hepatitis.

I thought of it as I read of a crippling sickness that attacked the helpless residents of Little Elk Creek near Elkton . . . helpless, until they successfully sued a manufacturer who had dumped his toxic waste into the creek.

And I thought of the massive counter-attack that you and I must wage to save our troubled waters when I was made to realize the arrogance of the polluter by the following statement:

"Big business is not concerned with what's best for the environment," Iowa congressman Berkley Bedell told a gathering of the Outdoor Writers of America last summer. "It is concerned with what is best for the interest of the stockholders."

You must realize that it is more profitable to pollute than it is to spend money to correct pollution." This is my concern. I surely hope that it is also your concern. Our bay depends on it.

Red Hamer
West Chester, Pa.
and
Oxford, Md.

NORTH
CHESAPEAKE

PRETTY AS A PICTURE — motor yacht Casablanca (left) framed by driftwood in Rogue's Harbor, Elk River.

HERE THEY COME! — National steeplechase races at Fair Hill, Maryland near the head of the Bay offers pretty railbirds, lots of green open country, vibrant silks and parimutuel machines. Up to 10,000 pack the stands for the late May hunt meeting.

FLAG WAVING AFFAIR—North East, Maryland Water Festival is typical of the fun events that permeate the Bay. Parade (above) kicks off the day, then kite man does his stuff at head of the North East River.

NORMAN ROCKWELL painted scenes like this all of his life—on "the island" near the top of the North East River.

STORM COMING up the bay to picturesque North East, Maryland Creek, northern tongue of the North East River. Upper Bay Museum, formerly Harvey's Fish House, sits at the mouth.

9

ELK NECK STATE PARK just south of North East, Maryland is a paradise for wild flower lovers, board surfers and beach fishermen. Hundreds camp at altitudes up to 200 feet over the Elk and North East Rivers. Jelly fish do not move this far north to mar swimming in the hot summer months.

CANDIDATE for "most beautiful cove on the Bay" is Rogue's Harbor (right) located a mile northeast of Turkey Point on the Elk River.

THE HIGH AND THE MIGHTY—Millard E. Tydings Memorial Bridge, Havre de Grace, Maryland, runs a mile long and 100 feet over the Susquehanna River. Scientists theorize that thaws of three ice ages tens of thousands of years ago flowed down the Susquehanna from Pennsylvania and flooded into a low lying area 190 miles long to form the Chesapeake Bay, America's largest estuary.

CECIL COUNTY ANTIQUITY—St. Mary Anne's Church in North East, Maryland dates to 1742, but the unmarked Indian grave stones on its grounds precede this Dutch-styled church. In 1718, Queen Anne of England presented communion vessels, a Bible and a book of common prayer to the parish before they built the church. These gifts are used today in special services.

BRITISH LANDING—That water below is the Elk River where Gen. Billy Howe landed 15,000 British troops in August, 1777. They marched into Pennsylvania and defeated Washington's Army in the Battle of the Brandywine on Sept. 11. Photo was made from Elk Neck Road, two miles from landing.

OLD FISH EYES — The fish are jumping at sundown off Tolchester, Maryland, and nobody is more attentive than Harry the Heron.

SOUNDS OF THE ISLANDS — Steel drum band from St. Croix entertains at Schaefer's Dock on Chesapeake and Delaware Canal . . . Passing ship (below) enchants dinner guests of the Canal House next door.

GILPIN'S FALLS BRIDGE on Route 272 near North East, Maryland is one of two covered bridges still standing in Cecil County. This one was built in 1860.

WASHINGTON COLLEGE—a sweep of green and colonial brick graces Chestertown, Maryland. It is the oldest college on the Eastern Shore and is named after George Washington who spoke at its founding in 1782.

SPRING HAS SPRUNG — classic Maryland colonial brick farm house in Kennedyville is strikingly set off by a broad field of green and a touch of yellow.

RARE PAIR — Canvasbacks cruise through McDaniels Yacht Basin on the North East River, but they are a scarce species of duck in Maryland and it is illegal to kill them there. Pollution has wiped out their favorite food, wild celery grass; and what pollution has not accounted for, Canadian geese have, by yanking the grass out by its roots. Tens of thousands of canvasbacks were hunted in season on the nearby Susquehanna, but no more.

ALL THAT GLITTERS is a golden way of life for boatmen on the Bay, no less for the tugboat operator (above) crusing south past Tolchester, Maryland.

JETTY marks the entrance from the Bay to the historic fishing village of Rock Hall, Maryland (below).

SHREWSBURY CHURCH—Three churches were built on this site, the first in 1692, this last one in 1832. Located south of Galena, Maryland on Route 213. Brig. General John Cadwalader, who shot out a man's teeth for disparaging his friend George Washington, is buried here with an inscription by Thomas Paine etched on his grave stone.

CHIMNEYS HAVE IT—Sign of affluence in colonial times was the number of chimneys in a home in which "Duck Hollow" across from the Kitty Knight House, Georgetown, Maryland, abounds. Kitchen of this lovely residence was built in 1790. Center of the structure was burned in 1813 by the marauding British when Kitty Knight, then 37, could not get her broom across the street in time to put out the flames.

SASSAFRAS GLITTER—glistening through the hollyhocks that grace the back lawn of the Kitty Knight House in Georgetown, Maryland is the snake-like Sassafras River, one of the real beauties of the 47 major rivers flowing into the Bay.

OYSTER SEEDING . . . Former oyster buy boat Rebecca Forbush power hoses shells into Miles River in 1980. She became tour boat out of Annapolis in 1985.

COMMERCIAL or sport fishing knows no geographical boundaries on the Bay. In the early spring Charlestown, Maryland fishermen on the northern most North Eas River check their nets for perch.

TEA DUMPERS — Red blooded Chestertown, Maryland colonists row their barge to the skipjack Stanley Norman to confiscate English tea and dump it into the Chester River. The ceremony occurs late in May every year with thousands watching on shore. It is the focal point of a weekend-long bash to commemorate the 1774 dumping of tea from the ship, Geddes. The hostile act by Chestertown natives came in sympathy for Boston tea dumpers, who had their port closed by the British. The Bostonians destroyed the tea because the English had suddenly put a tax on it.

THE STORY OF KITTY KNIGHT confronting the British in the War of 1812 and beating out the flames of two houses which later were joined to form the Kitty Knight House (above) is well known. What is not so well known is that Kitty's ghost roams the property.

OBSERVED by both employees and guests of the inn, Kitty's famous rocking chair has been seen to rock without provocation. Restaurant hostess (below) poses as Kitty.

ACCORDING to inn owner Howard Fellows, Kitty frightened a gardener out of his wits eight years ago by appearing in a white, wispy dress under an archway (the archway is seen next to the Queen St. sign above). The otherwise stout-hearted fellow dropped his tools, ran off in great fright and never returned to the garden.

KITTY was buried in 1855 at "Old Bohemia" Church (below). The raised grave stone tablet can be seen under the second window from the rear. Church, built in 1704, is located in Warwick, Maryland.

CENTREVILLE, MARYLAND is well named. It is the center of everything in Queen Anne's County. The court house (circa 1791) in this county seat is the oldest in continuous use in Maryland. The court house green (below) provided the scene for a visit from Prince Richard of Gloucester, England in May, 1980 as reporters from the local newspaper Record-Observer (top) observed, and the town bell tower (right) sparkled.

CENTREVILLE joins a long list of Eastern Shore communities noted for their beautifully maintained colonial homes and the one at left is a notable example, located on the right side of Liberty Street coming in from the north.

TURKEY POINT LIGHT HOUSE sits on an 80-foot cliff overlooking the whirling confluence of the North East, Elk and Susquehanna Rivers and the Chesapeake Bay. Fannie May Salter, the only lady lighthouse keeper in America, lit her oil and electric lamps here from 1925 through 1948. The light is now battery operated. Fannie May saved a man's life in the shadow of the lighthouse in 1942. A freak wind capsized the canoe of Richard Feister of Coatesville, Pa. He could not swim, but luckily grabbed a fish stake. She put in calls to three locations and hours later, when all seemed lost, a motor boat answering her call came over from White Crystal Beach to pluck the man from the late spring waters.

THE RIDGE (and the lighthouse) can be seen from the Elk River side of Turkey Point (right).

SAILBOAT cuts a pretty figure along the back waters of the Bohemia River. 17th century map maker Augustine Herrman built two homes within a few hundred yards of this spot, but eventually both were destroyed by fire.

UPPER
EASTERN SHORE

HORSES AT HARRIS CREEK at Old McDonalds Farm near Claiborne, Maryland.

FISHING FOR BLUES at Claiborne on the Eastern Bay.

PLANTATION ENTRANCEWAY to "Three Chimneys" at Royal Oak near St. Michaels.

31

HAVEN IN STORMS (spiritual and nautical) is lovely Old Wye Church (circa 1721) and Shaw Bay at the head of the Wye River.

APPLE OF A CAMERA'S EYE—Old Wye Oak gets its tummy rubbed by a couple of active boys as early morning sun lights up its spring growth like a lantern. Last summer 90 MPH winds whipped through Wye Mills, tiny Maryland village where the 440-year-old oak is located, but the 50 cables installed to hold America's oldest white oak together held up. At right, Maryland Governor Harry Hughes chats with relatives of Iran hostages after placing yellow ribbon around famed state tree. Tiny one-room schoolhouse near tree was built in 1720.

ANCIENT CHURCH, MODERN ART—Ruins of White Marsh Church (circa 1790), final resting place of Robert Morris, who built Oxford, Maryland into a dynamic port of trade. Oxford turned to weeds after his fatal boating accident at the age of 40, but his son grew to prominence and financed the American Revolution. Church ruins are located along Route 50 between Easton and Cambridge.

MUTE TESTIMONY—Mute swans, at 35 pounds, are the heaviest birds that fly. The pair above were photographed at sunrise along Hunting Creek across the Miles River from St. Michaels. On the fly, they arch their wings over their back, a posture designed to appear imposing to their enemies. They have been known to drag potential predators such as foxes into the water to drown.

CYGNET or baby swan takes a leisurely cruise with mom on Shaw Bay at the mouth of the Wye East River (above). Mute swans are seen in St. Michaels only in summer and are replaced by whistling swans in October. Most mutes are banded about the neck with transmitters so naturalists can check their nests for offspring. At right huge swan takes off like a Boeing 707 lands, with at least three splats on the water with its racing feet before becoming airborne.

WILLIAM PENN SPOKE HERE—
Third Haven Meeting House, built upon
the banks of the Tred Avon in 1684 and
now located in downtown Easton, Maryland, is the oldest frame house of worship
in America.

BLUE HERON patiently waits for his
lunch to appear in a tributary of the Tred
Avon River at corner of Route 33 and
Easton bypass (at right).

BLACKWATER WILDLIFE REFUGE——a stream, a setting sun and quietude, in Dorchester County, Maryland.

ROBERT MORRIS INN—pride of the colonial Bay port of Oxford, Maryland. Inn was formerly the house of its namesake, built in 1710. Morris' son became financier of the American Revolution.

OLDEST PRIVATELY OWNED FERRY SERVICE in America makes dozens of trips between Oxford and Bellevue, Maryland every day. The long run started in 1683, the year before Oxford was actually laid out as a town.

GUY, GIRL, SUNSET, SAILBOAT—in Town Park, Oxford, overlooking the Tred Avon River.

CHESAPEAKE BAY MARITIME MUSEUM director R. James Holt (above) views St. Michaels Harbor aboard the beautifully restored bugeye Edna E. Lockwood built in 1889. Refurbished Hooper Strait Lighthouse is at top right, and "old face" of museum at far right.

AUTHOR James A. Michener (right) whose best selling novel **Chesapeake** has brought droves of sight-seers to the Eastern Shore.

THE LOOK OF EASTON, "colonial capital of Maryland's Eastern Shore," is embodied in this superbly preserved brick building (left), the home of the Historical Society of Talbot County. The building (circa 1809) also is the showcase for the prize winning gardens (below) of the Talbot County Garden Club.

WEBLEY, SHOW PLACE WITH A SPIRIT—This ultimate Eastern Bay mansion is so much like a lovely lady: appealing from every angle. Indeed she can catch a sailor's sharp eye all the way from Bloody Point Bar Light at the south end of Kent Island. Webley grew up as a plantation about 1730, but her name changed to Mary's Delight in 1805 because John Kersey's daughter Mary had a very great love for the place with the picture sunsets. Mary's spirit still roams the grounds, according to owner David L. Baker.

Dr. Absolom Thompson lived here in 1830 and made his rounds barefoot and bareback upon a mule in the country around Wittman, Md. His practice grew so large that he turned the great house into the Eastern Shore's first hospital. It had returned to a private residence by 1924 when two wings were added. The place today has 10 fireplaces and a superb porch behind the pillars from which to dine and enjoy the sun setting over the Chesapeake.

EASTERN BAY coastline known as Bayside or Bay One Hundred, Talbot County, Maryland.

45

LOG CANOE RACERS take over the Miles River every July 4 weekend. Magic (above and upper left) wins the event, but her crew had to clamber onto springboards to keep her righted. Note kite atop the old racer's foremast and plastic window in mainsail so helmsman Jimmy Wilson can have a clear view. Boat was built in 1892 and has won more than 10 Governor's Cup races. Tandem boats at left are Jay Dee, Isle of Lark and Spirit of Wye Town (left to right).

FACES OF THE MIGHTY CHOPTANK—Spill from waste disposal plant in Cambridge, Md. closed beach (below) to bathers in the summer of '80. This shot was taken in the spring. River is 1.7 miles wide at this point, and above, where angler fishes against backdrop of Cambridge beach houses. In Greensboro, Md., 24 miles upriver, kids enjoy swimming hole known as "Hocum."

SECOND AVENUE, QUEENS-
TOWN—Once a booming ship-
ping port with five hotels and a
railway that went to the main dock,
now a quiet fishing village.

BOWLINGLY (1733)—James Bowling, a merchant, built this imposing mansion on the Queenstown Creek from which one can see 20 miles
into the Chesapeake. It later became a resort hotel. Gracing its grounds is
the largest pin oak in America.

49

A LITTLE BIT OF HEAVEN is what settlers found when they sailed down the Little Choptank into Fishing Creek and south into Church Creek (left). They built the Old Trinity Episcopal Church (below) on its banks in 1675, now the oldest active church in America. Maryland Gov. Thomas King Carroll and many Revolutionary War heroes are buried there. Most of the people who live in Church Creek are of direct English descent.

BOAT BUILDER JIM RICHARDSON contemplates the finish of his bugeye Jenny Norman (stern partially visible). Richardson's family, always boat builders, came over from England in 1650. Out of his boat yard in Lloyds, Maryland near Cambridge have come the replicas of many colonial ships, and the Spocott Windmill (left). The Chesapeake buy boat (bottom) was built by his son in law Tom Howell and named *Mr. Jim* in Richardson's honor. Richardson worked alongside his father as a teenager, which is how his latest boat got her name. "Jenny Norman was a friend of my father's," he recalled. "I heard him say to himself once, 'She would have been a joy to live with.' Well, I hope this boat will be a joy to live with, too." Richardson was the prototype for the early boat builders in Michener's novel *Chesapeake*.

BATHING BEAUTY — Common white egret finds a perch to sun herself and observe the boats in a cove at Tilghman Creek off the Miles River.

TOLSON COCKEY'S BOAT BARN — Tilghman Creek, Maryland.

TWO BUMPS ON A LOG—discussing latest Eastern Shore gossip.

DONALD AND FRIEND — Ducks are so comfortable in St. Michaels they don't migrate. This boat, owned by the author, was so long in the Harbor the two characters discussing the evening news apparently mistook it for an island. Longfellows and Quarter-Deck Restaurants are in background.

BOTTOM'S UP — Another view of the friendly fowl from the aft cabin below through the transparent hatch, at 7 A.M.

WATER COLORIST and the hollyhocks of St. Michaels. The town is a delightful mix of boats, antiquity and flower gardens.

FOURTH OF JULY WEEKEND in St. Michaels Harbor is a hell's a popping good time on the water. Torrid sun rises behind excursion ship (lower right) as Hooper Strait Light winks an early good morning to kick off festivities which include crabbing off Navy Point (below), setting off sparklers (above) and watching fireworks rise over Miles River Yacht Club (above right).

MILES RIVER SUPERINTENDENT—Mother osprey keeps an eye peeled on her offspring and the other on sailor to make sure he's doing his job right. Fish hawks migrate to places as far away as Argentina for the winter.

TAYLOR ISLAND has deep roots because boats—the major mode of transportation in colonial times—could get there via the Bay, Little Choptank River and Slaughter Creek. The Chapel of Ease (above), was built in 1707, and the first school of Dorchester County, Maryland (right), was erected in 1700.

GROUND AND PORCH LEVEL VIEW of the widow's walk at the Stapleforte Neild farm house on Taylor's Island. The water view is of a seven-mile stretch of the Chesapeake over to the Calvert Cliffs. Former owner Judge Levi D. Travers used the high perch to observe whether his field hands were tending the crops properly.

LONG PORCH—for the active pacer, at the T.A. Howell estate on the Choptank.

"PRETTIEST OF THE YEAR" is what Sharon Duffy called this Choptank River sunset. Sharon lives at the corner of Oak Street and Riverside Drive in Cambridge, Maryland, the spot from which this photograph was made on June 17, 1980.

61

MILES RIVER CRABBER — "I was a farmer. I was a carpenter for duPont. Now I've been crabbin' and oysterin' for 20 years. I'd rather do this than anything. I'm working for myself and at my age (70) I'm too old to be bossed around . . . And if there's a depression I know my next meal's out there in the water."

— Roland Lomax, St. Michaels, Md.

Lomax takes his wood fishing boat across the Miles River to Hunting Creek almost every morning at 4:30, lays out trot lines of 500 and 800 yards. They are baited with eels that, he says, "stink real good. That's the way the crabs like 'em." He uses a steel net to scoop the crabs off the bait and dump them into bushel baskets. He sorts the hard and soft shell crabs later with hand tongs. Lomax's morning vigil in the Eastern Shore waters is a study in exquisite color and wildlife as osprey, mute swans and deer pleasantly distract him. "The deer not only come down to the water for a drink," he said, "they go in for a swim. They swim right quick. You'd have to open up your boat full throttle to keep up with them."

WICOMICO ORANGE — The setting sun on the swamp (right) south of Salisbury, Maryland on Riverside Drive changes from yellow to purple to orange to orange red on a clear day. See a string of lights? That's a tugboat pulling a barge.

LOWER
EASTERN SHORE

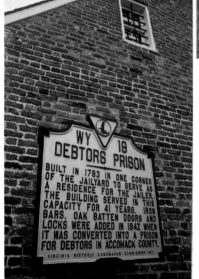

OLDEST COURT RECORDS in America, dating to 1632, were kept in this Eastville, Virginia court house (built in 1731) until the new court house was built. Declaration of Independence was read at its door on August 13, 1776.

OLD BRICK—this debtors prison in Accomac, Virginia was originally built in 1783 as a house for the town jailer.

EYRE HALL near Eastville was completed in 1759 and the rambling white frame house and grounds which front on the Cherrystone Creek have been in the Eyre family ever since.

SUNKEN MEMORIES along the cypress swamp
in Nassawango Creek near Snow Hill, Maryland.

SOMERS COVE HARBOR, CRISFIELD, MARYLAND

CRISFIELD, CRABBING CAPITAL OF THE BAY, IF NOT THE WORLD—Crabber masters back fin hold on crab (left) at loading dock of Milbourne Oyster Co. . . . Below, Bill Daley, of Tangier Island, empties his catch into vat . . . Cooker John Henry prepares steam bath . . . Below left, fishermen prepare for a 7 a.m. departure from West Main Street dock.

THE WHITTLERS OF SACKERTOWN ROAD

AMERICA'S FOREMOST DECOY MAKER—Lem Ward (above), of Sackertown Road, Crisfield, Md., together with his late brother Steve, carved, sanded and painted 25,000 decoys in their legendary careers that began in 1918. Forty years ago they would get $5 for the pair of pintails shown here. Recently a pair of their canvasbacks brought $2,500.

"My work became more valuable after my stroke," said Lem, now 84. The Ward Museum was established in their honor in Salisbury and a commemorative stamp is now in circulation, entitled, "Ward Brothers—A Legacy to Maryland." Now confined to a wheelchair because of a leg amputation, Lem spends his time signing remarques on the stamp proofs.

ELMER RIGGIN (above), 79, former hunting pal and neighbor of Lem Ward, has been building model boats of the Chesapeake nearly all of his life. They include skipjacks, bugeyes, oyster buy boats, 3-masted schooners and work boats. "I got a quarter for them when I was a little kid," Riggin said. Now his models sell for between $150 and $650. A hardy soul, Riggin had his first job at 8 and owned a skipjack at 14.

FEET FIRST—Cypress tree shows you its whole foot on the Nassawango Creek just off the Pocomoke River where the waters are murky, almost bottomless and fraught with long-snouted gar fish. Nearest town is Snow Hill, Maryland.

CRISFIELD CRAB—Two girls who just returned from an excursion to Smith Island via the type of boat seen coming into Crisfield, Maryland in background, enjoy a crab delicacy in Captain's Galley Restaurant overlooking Tangier Sound.

SCENES FROM SMITH ISLAND—12 miles across Tangier Sound from Crisfield lies an island (right) founded in 1608 by the legendary Capt. John Smith. Even today there is no government there, no police department, cars run around with no mufflers (the salt air eats 'em right up), all roads are one way (whichever way you happen to be going) and the 650 inhabitants—mostly named Tyler or Evans—are very friendly.

THE CRAB SHACKS of Smith Island, Maryland.

WORKING AT THE MAIN INDUSTRY.

MAIN STREET—"This is a unique place with unique people, some people say," said Clara Tyler, the lady on the bike. "But we're just like anybody else. We are just a place (and people) surrounded by water." The Smith Islander is a bit more patriotic than the average mainlander. There are American flags and yellow ribbons (in honor of the Iran hostages) everywhere.

OFFICIAL GREETER

RETIRED CRISFIELD WORKBOAT—"Was it Mr. Trumpy who said you never finish working on a boat. When you do, the man just comes and takes it away."

—Jim Richardson, boat builder.

WEATHER BEATEN—West Main Street, Crisfield, Maryland.

LARGEST BUGEYE—82-foot Robert L. Webster on exhibition at Janes Island State Park near Crisfield (at right).

CLEANING FISH along Wachapreague Inlet, sport fishing capital of Virginia Eastern Shore.

SEA GULLS FEEDING off clam shells on conveyer belt at American Original plant, Willis Wharf, Virginia.

SEA BASS (right) is brought in regularly by Wachapreague, Virginia anglers fishing the nearby Atlantic.

LOW TIDE at Box Tree Landing, Machipongo, Virginia.

DOWNTOWN FISHING—at the Wicomico River spillway in Salisbury, Maryland city park. The stream offers blue gill, bass and good old carp.

POPLAR HILL MANSION—oldest house (circa 1820) in Salisbury. Fire wiped out everything built earlier in Eastern Shore's largest city.

LOWER WESTERN SHORE
ON THE ROAD TO . . .

. . . *COLONIAL WILLIAMSBURG, VIRGINIA.*

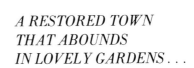

A RESTORED TOWN
THAT ABOUNDS
IN LOVELY GARDENS . . .

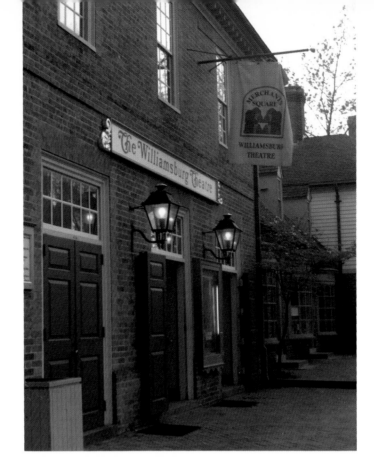

. . . CULTURE

THE WILLIAMSBURG THEATRE

. . . BUILT
TO TOUR

GOVERNOR'S MANSION—one of the finest pieces of architecture in America, built in 1720. Patrick Henry and Thomas Jefferson, the first two governors of the Virginia colony, plus seven royal governors, lived here.

OLD CAPITOL BUILDING of the Virginia Colony.

. . AND PLACES TO PHOTOGRAPH.

. . . ARCHITECTURE TO STUDY

CARTER'S GROVE PLANTATION in the woodlands of Williamsburg, Virginia has been called "the most beautiful house in America." Washington, Jefferson and later Winston Churchill were entertained in this mansion built 250 years ago. An Indian massacre of the Jamestown settlers took place near here in 1622. The estate overlooks the James River.

GLOUCESTER, VIRGINIA
court house square is one of
the most charming seats of government in the Bay area. Pil-
lared building is courthouse
built in 1776.

VAN TAVERN, a landmark in historic Yorktown, Virginia since 1722. For 133 years the tavern was a leading place of public entertainment.
was destroyed by fire in Civil War days when a nearby ammunition magazine blew up. Rebuilt on its original foundations, the tavern today
ves as an antique shop.

JOHN LENNON of Beatles fame purchased Poplar Grove Plantation house and dependencies (above) and mill (right page) in 1980 — just two months before he was fatally shot in New York City. Mansion house was built in 1750. The 22-acre estate is located near Mathews, Va.

SHELTERED ANTIQUE — Clyde W. Hudgins, Sr. of Poplar Grove Road near Mobjack Bay, takes good care of this 1900 two seat horse surrey. It's mid-May and thermometer on the barn already reads 90 degrees.

PAINTER'S DREAM—This mill on an estuary of Mobjack Bay near Mathews, Virginia is the last of the Chesapeake's tide mills. The wooden wheel turns one way when the tide comes in, flows the other way when the tide goes out. Grain was ground here for Washington's troops during the siege of Yorktown in 1781. For historical and aesthetic reasons, it is one of the most photographed mills in existence.

MORNING WATERING—The Nelson House in Yorktown, Virginia where Tom Nelson, Jr. lived. He signed Declaration of Independence, served as wartime governor of Virginia and commanded the Virginia militia during the siege of Yorktown in 1781.

CAVE MAN—Lord Cornwallis was forced to move his headquarters to this cave on Water Street, Yorktown, a few feet from the scene at right, such was the intensity of the heavy shelling from the American and French forces. Cornwallis and the British surrendered October 19, 1781, thus forever ending the Revolutionary War.

WHAT A DIFFERENCE a couple of hundred years make. British troops were thrown back by a storm here on the beach of the York River in 1781, and surrendered to Washington's American and French forces to end the Revolutionary War. The remains of the British ship Charon, a 116-foot frigate that was sunk in the Battle of Yorktown, was recovered in the summer of 1980.

JAMES FORT, JAMESTOWN, VIRGINIA— How America's first permanent English settlement looked a year after the landing in 1607. As militia drills below, church is being completed above and at extreme right. Sections of the three tiny ships that brought over the first 105 settlers—Discovery, Godspeed and Susan Constant (in drydock)—are shown below.

NEW POINT COMFORT LIGHTHOUSE, where Mobjack Bay meets the Chesapeake Bay. World War II beach invasion practice was held on these beaches of Virginia's western shore.

MENHADEN FISHING BOAT moves out of Reedville, along Virginia's Northern Neck, in search of the most plentiful fish in the ocean. Menhaden fish are ground up in the factories in Reedville and the oil product is used in manufacturing linoleum and soap. The ships unload their cargo all hours of the night and the billowy white smoke rising from the factories can be seen for miles.

OLD VIRGINIA CHURCHES—St. John's Episcopal Church (left) in Richmond, where Patrick Henry shouted: "Give me liberty, or give me death" in 1775 at the second Virginia Convention. Below, St. Stephens Episcopal Church in Heathsville, founded in 1653 as Chickacone Parish.

STATE CAPITOL of Virginia (above) houses one of the world's oldest representative legislatures. Richmond is the former capital of the Confederacy.

OLDEST (CIRCA 1686) HOUSE IN RICHMOND—On exhibition are manuscripts by poet Edgar Allan Poe in this shrine-museum in memory of the great poet.

RICHMOND, VIRGINIA, near the head waters of the James River, is a city of statues and museums and may look its best in the spring as the sun gives the young leaves a sparkling tinsel effect. The Washington Statue (right), a likeness of poet Edgar Allan Poe (below, left) who spent his childhood and young manhood in the Virginia capital; and (below, right), the Museum of the Confederacy.

TALLEST LIGHTHOUSE IN AMERICA stretches 165 feet at Cape Henry, Virginia. Beacon is visible for 19 miles. Picture was made from site of the old Cape Henry lighthouse which was built in 1792. It served until 1881 when this one was lighted.

WHERE IT ALL BEGAN — Cape Henry Memorial marks the spot where Captain Christopher Newport and 104 colonists from England buried a cross in Virginia sand after landing April 26, 1607. They spent four days here and named the spot Cape Henry after the Prince of Wales. The three small ships that brought them — Discovery, Godspeed and Susan Constant — then took off for the James River where they founded Jamestown. This picture was made just after six o'clock on an April morning.

NORFOLK, VIRGINIA takes on a vibrant coat of color in the spring. The Gardens-By-The-Sea come alive (left and below) with tulips and azaleas everywhere. Above, the boxwood garden of Adam Thoroughgood House. Built in 1636, it is the oldest standing brick house in America, located in Virginia Beach.

NORFOLK, VIRGINIA—a city built on sand, and oh, what beautiful beaches it makes! For an office worker, view of the boats going by counts for an added benefit.

HARBORFEST at downtown Norfolk waterfront attracts thousands in May, 1980. Brig Unicorn, which appeared in the movie, *Roots*, was one of many tall ships on exhibition. Below, railbirds grab a little violin music at dockside.

CALYPSO—ocean going exploratory ship of famed Captain Jacques Cousteau, on exhibition at Norfolk Harborfest '80.

UPPER WESTERN SHORE

CHESAPEAKE BAY BRIDGE—4.3 miles of steel girders.

SANDY POINT, north of Annapolis, takes an artistic turn. State park is one of the most popular beaches on the Maryland Chesapeake.

BALTIMORE'S INNER HARBOR, a picture of spring-like tranquility as viewed from atop Federal Hill.

STUBBY CANNONS protect Fort McHenry's front lawn overlooking Patapsco River. Excavation has begun for two ships sunk that early morning in 1814 when the fort's defenders kept the American flag flying high despite a rocketing bombardment by the British. School is out on whether vessels are British or American.

CONSTELLATION, America's vintage warship (circa 1797) in drydock for $2.1 million in repairs at Fort McHenry shipyard. Boat builder Jim Richardson, 73, who reshaped her 50-foot plus bowsprit at his Lloyds, Md. boat yard, declared: "No way you could say she is pretty. Maybe she is pretty like a hog, or a cook stove or whatever."

HUES OF THE SEVERN—On a clear day you can see forever, or at least down river into the Chesapeake where hundreds of sails dot the skyline. That's where the fast action lies. For a more romantic setting you might choose an upriver tack past cliffs and into small bays. Two boats (right), keeping beat like one heart, return at day's end from such an outing.

IT'S SUNSET TIME on the Severn River Bridge (Route 301). The lower photo was taken several minutes after the sun descended and after the sailboats moved to the middle of the scenic river. Round Bay is upstream.

ANNAPOLIS SHORT TOUR—Top left, Playhouse Theatre, at alley's end; Top right, two middies find Main Street; Bottom left, Governor's Mansion; Bottom right, Maryland State House, nation's oldest, begun in 1772.

FIT FOR A BRIDE—With suggestions from architecturally inclined Thomas Jefferson along the way, William Paca finished off this in-town plantation house (below) for his bride in 1765. Today the Paca House—named after the three-term governor of Maryland—is one of the showplaces of Annapolis.

Marked for demolition, the mansion was saved by Historic Annapolis, Inc. in 1965 and restored to its colonial elegance; the gardens were discovered after removal of 11 feet of debris. The rear of the main house is seen below. The gardens above are viewed from the third floor of the house.

JUMPING FOR JOY and for doggy treats is Corker, a three-month old Lhasa Apso, complete with life jacket. Corker, Jimmy Nardo, 8, his brother Louis, 10, (at left), mom and dad sailed from this Mears Marina slip the next day in the second Annapolis to Bermuda race. The Lancaster, Pa. couple had never sailed in the ocean, so it was a thrill all the way.

ANNAPOLIS TO BERMUDA RACE—Spinnakers pop behind a "just right" breeze at Buoy 77, Polly Point where the Severn River breaks into the Chesapeake. This was the starting line for a race timed to start one day after the beginning of the Newport, R.I. to Bermuda race. The Annapolis crews hoped to make the run in 3½ days, but the 753-mile journey required seven days. One boat lost a mast, another leaked badly. But all hands arrived safely.

AMERICAN PIE skipper Gary Van Hoven (right) waves goodbye coming out of Severn.

MARYLAND DOVE — Jim Richardson-built replica of the pinnace that brought settlers to Maryland in 1634, shown tied up at Bromo's Wharf, along high banks of St. Mary's City.

MARYLAND'S FIRST STATE HOUSE, built in 1676 at St. Mary's City at cost of 300,000 pounds of tobacco, is shown in reconstructed state below. Theatre group portrays St. Mary's colonists during the summer (bottom). Girl (right) peers through State House window for view of "sedition trial" staged by colonial players.

MILITIA DRILL on the grounds of the Surratt House and Tavern.

SURRATT'S TAVERN in Clinton, Maryland is the scene of many Civil War period re-enactments by the Surratt Society. The town, formerly known as Surrattsville, is located about 10 miles southeast of Washington, D.C. The original tavern owner, Mary Surratt, was hanged for purportedly aiding John Wilkes Booth, the man who shot Lincoln. Evidence reveals she was implicated by a "forgetful drunk" and that the execution (the first of a woman in the U.S.) was a gross miscarriage of justice. She was regarded by her contemporaries as a "gentle and deeply religious woman." Her ghost reportedly still roams through Fort McNair where she was tried and hanged.

CIVIL WAR DOCTOR and his main surgical instrument. 113

SMOKE STACKS ARE IN STYLE below the Annapolis bridge (top). These belong to Liberia, Greece and Turkey. They are waiting for slips to open in Baltimore to deliver their oil.

TANKER SASSTOWN roars down the bay with Kent Island to her port.

TENDER brings the crew of Turkish freighter back to ship after a shopping spree in Annapolis

THOMAS POINT LIGHTHOUSE — the last of the manned lighthouses on the Bay. Located near mouth of the South River. National Historical Register lists the 104-year-old hexagonal house. It was automated in 1981. Coast Guard wanted to tear it down, but local residents said no.

STARBOUND, a 50-foot cruising topsail ketch, languishes off Navy Point, St. Michaels, July 4 weekend. But the charming 30-year-old boat is not accustomed to standing still. Gordon Stuermer, shown below (looking skyward) having a crab feast with guests, sailed her around the world with his wife, Nina (middle photo), from 1973 through 1976, wrote a book about it, called **Starbound,** and intends to make the trip again.

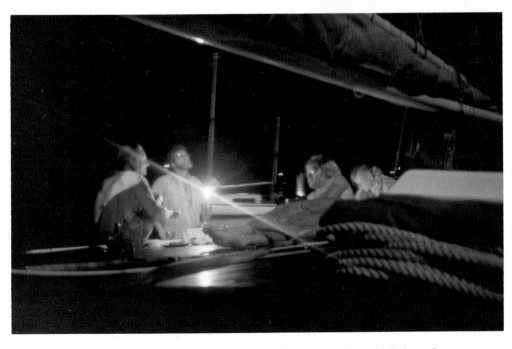

SUNDAY RUSH HOUR—Here comes the Weekend Navy (left) out of Back Creek, Annapolis.

LONDON TOWN PUBLIK HOUSE was constructed on the South River between 1744 and 1750. The inn was the center of activity of a thriving seaport. It was from here that Maryland's popular tobacco was carried to foreign ports. This was also a major stopping off place for travellers between Williamsburg and Philadelphia. The bustling town declined when Annapolis, its docks much closer to the Chesapeake, gained favor as a port. The ferry service which carried across river for journeys north or to the horse races in Annapolis suffered an accident in 1769 when the overloaded boat capsized and two people were drowned. London Town was also a port for slave ships.

CALVERT CLIFFS—A great place to play on the beach and to look for fossils if you don't mind hiking two miles through woods to get to this famed stretch of the Maryland Western Shore. Sharks' teeth and other fossils are 15 million years old.

COVE POINT LIGHTHOUSE, circa 1828, as pictured from a dinghy (above) and as seen in the background of Calvert Cliffs beachfront (left). 119

AN HISTORIC OCCASION

COMMENCEMENT at the U.S. Naval Academy in the Navy-Marine Corps Memorial Stadium provided a new twist on May 28, 1980 when the graduating class included women—55 of them, led by Elizabeth Anne Belzer who graduated with honors. 897 men received their commissions.

SUNDAY SCHOOL is held for midshipmen aboard destroyer Hancock
anchored in the Chesapeake at the mouth of the Severn.

JUST HOW HIGH IS A TALL SHIP?—High enough to make them open the jaws of the Woodrow Wilson Bridge as the Christian Radich—with admirers in abundance—wends her way down the Potomac River.

THE DANMARK, another tall ship of Danish ancestry, is photographed from atop the Woodrow Wilson Bridge against a backdrop of Old Alexandria, Virginia. Both the Radich and Danmark were on exhibition in late spring at the 1980 Washington, D.C. Harborfest. These incredibly beautiful and graceful clipper ships of old, reborn, often serve as training vessels for foreign navies.

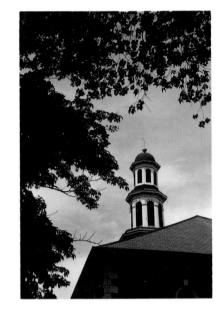

OLD ALEXANDRIA, VIRGINIA, a study in colonial brick restoration. Left, warm days of May bring out the roses at 611 Queen Street; Right, steeple of Christ Church (1773) where Washington and Lee worshipped; Lower right, Robert E. Lee's boyhood home where, from 1818 to 1825, he prepared for West Point; Bottom right, the Lloyd House where Lee first learned he had been chosen to lead the military and naval forces of Virginia in the Civil War. The Lloyd House, built in 1797, today is a library for Alexandria and Virginia history buffs.

MT. VERNON'S flowering arbors and breezeway afford a northern view of the beautiful, winding Potomac River.

WASHINGTON'S HOME as viewed from the north terrace. Nation's first president lived at Mt. Vernon, Virginia from 1754 to his death in 1799. Nine years before he died, he told a friend: "I would rather be at Mount Vernon with a friend or two about me than to be attended at the Seat of Government by the officers of state and the representatives of every power in Europe."

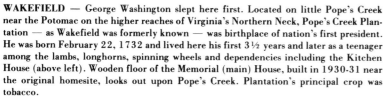

WAKEFIELD — George Washington slept here first. Located on little Pope's Creek near the Potomac on the higher reaches of Virginia's Northern Neck, Pope's Creek Plantation — as Wakefield was formerly known — was birthplace of nation's first president. He was born February 22, 1732 and lived here his first 3½ years and later as a teenager among the lambs, longhorns, spinning wheels and dependencies including the Kitchen House (above left). Wooden floor of the Memorial (main) House, built in 1930-31 near the original homesite, looks out upon Pope's Creek. Plantation's principal crop was tobacco.